Press regarding "Look Up at the Hawks," the program based on the writings of Ruth Morgan Smith:

Susan Stamberg (NPR): "It's interesting Ruth Morgan Smith's tone is never one of great frustration, or anger, yet her life was tough... what is that experience in Nebraska, of lying down and looking up at the hawks, circling?"
Vivian Smith: "There's this feeling of the vastness of everything, you feel very close to nature, and that's where Ruth drew a lot of strength..."

--National Public Radio
"All Things Considered"

"...The direct route Ruth's plain speech plainly spoken takes to our feelings is overwhelming and wonderful..."
--Kenneth Yellis, past Curator of Education
National Portrait Gallery, Smithsonian Institution

"...a personal journal of Ruth's life on the Nebraska plains in the 30's... 'Look Up at the Hawks' is connected through the talents of three generations..."
--The Washington Post

"...Ruth Smith was a hard-working, big-hearted Nebraska farmwoman. Many of Ruth Smith's eighty-four years were hard ones, particularly in the 1930's, when drought, dust storms and floods devastated her home and land. But she survived each setback with undiminished faith and good cheer. Ruth's story -- in her own words -- forms the basis of a fascinating story that combines the talents of three generations of the Smith family.
--Voice of America radio

BOSTWICK, NEBRASKA

Scale 2 inches to 1 mile

Township 1 North, Range 8 West of the 6th P. M.

PREC.

Bostwick — Town —

Nuckolls County — Township map showing layout of Bostwick with town and Morgan property

Landowner Henry C ? Morgan

LOOK UP AT THE HAWKS

AND THE UNIVERSE OVERHEAD

By Ruth Morgan Smith and Vivian Douglas Smith
Edited by Vivian Douglas Smith and Debi Smith

I lay me down
and look up at the hawks in the blue sky.
There is a high wind blowing,
and they poise with wings outspread,
almost perfectly still,
just tipping a little to one side,
then to the other,
to balance.
Now they swoop in a circle to climb higher
and balance again there.
Ah, me,
lying flat on the back,
and gazing up at the universe overhead,
one does discern the unimportance
of being important.

The ironing and mending
over at the house
shrink to insignificance
as I muse on what those graceful carefree hawks
would be missing
if there were ironing or mending
at home for them...

Ruth Morgan Smith
1894 – 1978

TO RUTH MORGAN SMITH

who took the time to put her thoughts and dreams into words, leaving us this legacy

PREFACE

Ruth Morgan Smith was my mother-in-law. Unknown to her family, during the 1930's and through the mid-1940's, Ruth was jotting down her thoughts and feelings about those harsh times as she lived them with her family on their farm in Bostwick, Nebraska. She gave those writings to me in 1972, and during the next seven years, I edited and arranged them.

Ruth was the eleventh of twelve children born to Leonidas Taylor Morgan and his wife, Mary Elizabeth Harvey Morgan, who had homesteaded in a covered wagon to the plains of Kansas in 1877. Ruth was born in 1894, after their move across the border line into Nebraska.

Because Ruth had such great admiration for her pioneering mother, I chose to unify her writings from the 30's in the form of letters to – conversations with – her mother. There were several actual letters; Mary Elizabeth and Leonidas had moved to Michigan in the 1920's to live with three of Ruth's sisters.

My husband, David, helped me with the chronological arrangement, and other family members also helped me fill in details where needed. Our daughter, Debi Smith, a professional singer, saw a new picture of her grandmother when she read what Ruth had written, and set some of her grandmother's words to music.

Ruth's story, by then involving three generations, was presented as a program at the Smithsonian's National Portrait Gallery and toured the Midwest in 1982. You will find additional details about the story's long journey at the end of this book.

We hope you will enjoy and find inspiration in Ruth Morgan Smith's "Look Up at the Hawks."

Vivian Douglas Smith

From Bostwick, Nebraska,
In the 1930's....

Dear Mother,

The youngest of your twenty-seven grandchildren, who is the youngest of my four children, started to school Monday. It seems so odd. I straighten up the house in the morning and it stays that way till 4:30 p.m. I lay the scissors down, and when I look for them again, there they are. And oh, it is so quiet! The first day, I caught myself singing or whistling at intervals, all day, to break up that strange continuity of stillness.

How I wish I could talk to you. Michigan is so far from Nebraska. In between the lines of your last letter, I can detect the loneliness that you feel during the day while my sisters there are away working at their jobs. It is said that trouble shared is cut in half; why shouldn't loneliness be so, too? Since you and I are kindred souls in that, perhaps I can bridge the distance between us by letter.

I have six pepper plants with fruit still to ripen and a few tomatoes that I treasure yet. That's how I'm herding cows today. Old Roan is the outstanding bully of them all. I doubt that she really likes tomatoes but she senses that I don't want her in them so that is where she will be. When my back is turned, she prods the other cows with her horns and literally pushes them toward the patch.

She is the great great great granddaughter of the cow you used to have, Mother. Remember? The one that got loose there in town, ran up to the banker's wash line on the hill and ate up the ladies' underwear that hung there?

Between times of cow chasing, I lay me down and look up the hawks in the blue sky. There is a high wind blowing and they poise with wings outspread, almost perfectly still, just tipping a little to one side, then to the other, to balance. Now they swoop in a circle to climb higher and balance again there. Do you suppose aircraft will ever be able to stop in the midst of flight and poise like hawks do?

Ah, me, lying flat on the back and gazing up at the universe overhead, one does discern the unimportance of being important. I confess to you that it's a lovely day and I'm not nearly so concerned about peppers and tomatoes as I am gratified to get out of doors for a day. I am like a creature of the fields caught up and held fast in a trap; a field mouse. I need a flash signal on the door: "Stop! Are your dishes done? Why are you going out this door?"

I secretly envy the woman with the orderly bump on her head well developed. She can no more help putting things away and keeping things neat than breathing. Housekeeping is her complex, just like it isn't my complex. More and more, I use this rationale as an excuse to ditch everything and walk out the door a free woman.

The ironing and mending shrink to insignificance as I muse on what those graceful carefree hawks would be missing if there were ironing or mending at home for them.

The cows have given me the slip. Just now I heard one of them bawl. I jumped up immediately, for that means she is lost from the rest of the herd. When she saw me, she gave a dash back into the dense thicket, and that is the last I have seen of any of them. I walk up to the lower gate to make sure there are no tracks going through it onto our neighbor's property, the Kiefers', and then I go up on the tall stump to scan about in every direction; but no cows. I come back to the tomato patch, their ultimate goal, and sit me down to wait till it pleases their majesties to return out of the wilderness.

Luther is across the river cutting what the grasshoppers and drought left for winter stock feed, so I had no lunch to get except for myself. I have eaten two sandwiches, four cookies, two apples and six tomatoes since breakfast. The tomatoes keep me from being thirsty.

I hear the cows now, over by the river, where they have gone to drink. I go to them, and I see they have disturbed a lone blue heron that rises majestically and sails in offended dignity up the river.

Now I will drive my charges to the lot at the barn, and turn to the next pleasant job of getting supper. I do like to cook when I am ravenously hungry. I caught a chicken when I turned them out this morning, so I can look forward to chicken, gravy, creamy mashed potatoes, bread, butter, jelly, applesauce, milk and tomato cups.

I must tell you about tomato cups: the other day, Luther Junior brought me a tomato and asked me to cut the top off of it. I did so, and watched curiously to see why the top must be off. He got a spoon and salt and scooped all the inside out and ate it like an orange. So the rest of us tried it, and welcomed a new way to eat tomatoes.

Tonight I will sleep like the dead; I always do after spending a day out of doors. I dislike to lie awake at night, for then little daytime worries that you can't shake off magnify into portentous night worries.

I just happened to remember it is Luther's birthday, so there will be cupcakes. This is once in his life Luther can't get any kick out of fried chicken. About last July, when we were getting such lovely rains, we decided it was safe to go ahead and have all his teeth out, and let the corn crop put them in again. But the rain suddenly stopped coming and the heat poured down on us relentlessly, until we have no corn crop and, alas, no teeth for Luther. No corn crop - no teeth.

I grind food up for him but things don't taste the same, he says. Luther was elected Sunday school superintendent. He forgets his teeth are gone and gives a toothless grin. A woman with teeth out shields her mouth with her hand; a man is unconscious of it. A feeling of protectiveness surges up in me. I mentally dare anyone to remark about it. I am a lioness - defensive, aggressive - for her mate or cub.

You read of distractions of modern times and life. Not many here. No radio - no telephone - no daily paper - no picture shows since long before the depression. It was hard to keep the correct time till I fell upon the plan to set the clock by sunrise or sunset, not from the Almanac, but from an occasional paper Luther gets from the newsstand. I overheard Betty say to her playmates yesterday, "No, it isn't four yet, because that clock is set by the correct sun time."

I kindle fires without kerosene. I put away pieces of board that contain resin, shave it in little sticks, light them and cover with fine twigs, and then my regular stove wood. But I hope I don't have to economize on matches and rub two sticks together like a Boy Scout.

In town, I sit in the car parked along Main Street, and watch the women's posture and their clothes. The young folks are nicely clad; the old folks wear shabby misfits. I see tenseness - singleness of purpose. Now I'd like to sit in a car on a city street.

Dust storms have made this the poorest spot in the U.S. Here you find all old model cars from the year '28 back to Model-T, still running. I refuse to worry about money. Dad always manages to bring home the bacon - or dried beef.

But I do worry about the health of my family. I just can't help it. I'm sure we have excellent health as a family, but I'm like the Quaker who called his sons to his deathbed and said, "All my life I've worried about things that never came to pass." Our family of six lived on nine dollars one month during the depression, and we can do it again if necessary. Oh, once in awhile I kick in the traces when we fall too far behind the Joneses, but not too often, thank heaven.

I never wanted nice clothes so badly in my life as the year Lena and I went to school at Northwestern in Chicago. I believe I would have gone without food to get them. So I can feel sorry for the city mothers who skimp on milk and eggs to keep the family dressed up to a certain standard.

The other day, while Luther was having a tire fixed, I overheard a group of farmers discussing the plight of a man who had shot himself from over-worrying. One man said, "Do you reckon that would be an easy way out?" Their consensus of opinion was that it was probably unsportsmanlike to those left behind.

Some who have the courage and the gas are getting out with their shirts on their backs. Others can't get away. God laid this out for a grazing country, and it isn't His headache if man plowed the virgin prairie up in his frenzy for wheat money.

The depression bugaboo is fading, but now we have crop failure one after another. Sometimes the farmers are glum; wheat is going by the board, worthless, this fall. Hundreds of acres of corn land around here were put in wheat because there was a fair crop of wheat last spring and it matured before the grasshoppers got in full swing. But now the wheat is very spotty and must be re-sown if there is to be any chance at all for a crop next spring. The corn crop is going and the wheat crop is going. Still I will not be discouraged; our offspring crop, Jane - David - Betty - Luther, is doing finely.

The old homestead looked very forlorn and dejected the other day when we passed it. Really, it is just a little worse than lots of other farms in this country right now. Every time I think I'm having a hard time, all I need to think about is your mammoth family and remember some of the hard times you tell about and mine are easy.

Mary Elizabeth Harvey Morgan. You came across the prairies in 1877, in your covered wagon, with no idea where or when you would be stopping. You saw a house with a light in it along the way, and a great surge of homesickness swept over you for all that you had left behind.

You came with four children, two boys, and two girls, the same as I have. You thought that was a nice sized family; and it was, and is. You settled, finally, on a barren, hilly farm in Kansas, which to this day has never produced but a meager living to any one family living on it. That rocky, deserted sod house, now in ruins, proved as a homestead to be prolific only in babies, because you had six more children there in Kansas.

Although you never planned the family increases, every one of us were loved impartially from the time you felt us near your heart. Mary. A hallowed name. To me, it would have seemed a hopeless struggle, but not to you. You said the happiest days of your life were those days on the farm when the children were small.

Across the border in Nebraska, where you went seeking better education for your children, you had two more; one of them, me. You remember I asked you once if you hadn't endowed me with a gypsy complex because I am always happiest and healthiest out of doors? And I have always remembered your answer: you told me that while you were carrying me in embryo, you used to go to the upstairs window looking south to the hills of Kansas and stand there gazing longingly in the direction of the homestead you had left.

Mrs. Kiefer was telling me the other day about the first time she saw you. She was a bride. Her husband said he wanted her to meet Mrs. Morgan. She said she expected to meet a worn, weary mother of six children. Instead, she was amazed to see a cheerful, rosy-cheeked woman, serene and composed. She said you were with her when Margaret, her third child, was born. She had asked how long you could stay, and you replied, "Why, as long as you need me." I wonder how many newborn babies were ushered into the world for neighbors with you standing vigil at the bedside, giving them their first bath with your capable hands?

Every Saturday night found your ten children bathed and in bed with ten pairs of shoes blacked with stove black, lined up against the wall. On Sunday morning, getting ready for church was an ordeal - but not even the time Johnny fell in the stock tank with his Sunday best on prevented the family from attending church, with Johnny immaculate. After that, though, Johnny was the last one to be dressed before getting in the carriage for church. One man told me the sweetest singing voice he ever heard was your voice in the choir of that little sod church where you taught Sunday school class.

Sheep were your main cash crop. One crop of wool, shipped to St. Louis, was lost when the firm went bankrupt, with the wool in their possession. You received ten dollars instead of a hundred dollars. Another time, Dad signed the bond for an irresponsible neighbor, who defaulted, and you were left to pay the several hundred dollars that were owed.

There was a blizzard came up while the two boys were herding sheep. Harvey wanted to go one way, John the other, and round them up. John, with a man's head on a youth's shoulders, insisted that they keep together. Dad, following the fence, found them with the help of the dog; they got sheep and boys safely home. Don't I know what you went through just waiting there in the sod house for them to get back.

You, with a rake and the dog, killed more than one rattler in those Kansas hills. I can imagine how you must have felt, with all those little naked feet running about the place. Do you remember, (your children do), the old icehouse on the farm where the kids were taken for a needed "spare-the-rod-and-spoil-the-child?"

Once, you said, you longed all winter for some white bread; there was no wheat flour, so there was only corn bread all that long, hard winter. You put hardboiled eggs in children's hands and sent them off to school. The eggs provided heat for their hands in the cold prairie winds and food for their lunch at noon. The feisty little Scots-Irish lady who came here from Ireland at age three, and who was your mother, came out to visit once. She fumed at the lukewarm irons heated by burning twisted hay for fuel.

Cholera, malaria, smallpox, typhoid, diphtheria, the plagues of that day, somehow you escaped them, and all twelve of your brood grew into adulthood.

Bostwick Hotel was the boarding house you ran, where Pearl and I were born. Eva and Pearl and I reminisce about washing the noon dishes after school, getting the cows back when they strayed to the bridge, hoeing weeds in the corn patch, and the "sparkin' settee" in the corner where we all did our courting. The house was full when the girls were all home for the summer. Most of the rooms were occupied, especially after a dance.

Dad would yell, "Girls, there'll be none of this dawdling in the morning! Kate, remember it's washday tomorrow!" I think the boys were in awe of Dad - he was little but mighty. After all, nine girls are a responsibility.

Dad ran a livery stable; you ran the boarding house and a few other things, too. When the other choir members wanted to put out one member, young, unmarried, pregnant, you wouldn't allow it.

She got her way? "She always did," says my sister, Pearl. When a neighbor who got drunk chased his wife with a shotgun, she came to you for protection. "Mother just went out and sent him home," says my sister, Eva. You never did approve of gambling and card playing, and when you got wind of a game down at the lumber yard and heard that John and Harvey were there, you simply went down and broke it up.

Mr. and Mrs. Harrison drove in for a little visit last week. I haven't seen them for twenty years. Mr. Harrison wanted to know if my mother still made her grown daughters step around, and he laughed when he asked it. I'm sure he was thinking of the night you came over and took us all home from the dance across the way.

Have you forgotten? "Turkey in the Straw!" I enjoyed the square dances the most; I wanted to know the intricate ones. You never woke when they played dreamy waltzes or peppy two-steps, but the square dances riled you. I don't know why. You stood white-faced in the doorway and called, "Eva - Ruth - Pearl - Kathryn." Kate thought she was immune because she was with her betrothed. I had a girlfriend; I tried to squeeze behind her out of sight. But my name was called, too. We all filed meekly out across the street, home and to bed. But after that, we were needles and pins; whenever the square dances were played, we watched the door.

The afternoon naps were a constant in your life. "Forty winks," you called them. I can see you now in the chair in Dad's office that leaned back. You would sit down and go right to sleep. Five minutes later, you were up and on the go again.

The boarders came and went, ten of them at any given time. Life started getting better. There was a Ford now, and a pump in the sink, and a wash machine with a gasoline motor.

Of all your boarders, Miss Deal is the one whom we remember. Miss Deal taught piano, and that was the way she paid her board, with piano lessons. I can't thank you enough for the music lessons you gave me from Miss Deal. During the two years I taught in the country school, they were so helpful, then and now. David begs me to play most every night. I would rather he would learn to play himself. I can always get a bucket of water willingly if I will play. Pearl remembers the lessons too, but she never learned the notes (I wonder if you knew that?). She memorized the tunes from hearing all us older children practicing. I don't play difficult songs, but I got a book of classical pieces simplified for easy rendition and I think that gives my children a taste for good music.

We like to think that here in Bostwick we've had the best Christmas music programs around. My husband, Luther, always looking for perfection, likes to bring in new things, new ideas. Jane remembers the advice he always gave: "Dream it - see it - make it better." One year Jane brought in branches to decorate. "See," he said, "That's different. Nobody's done that here before." Luther leads the choir; Luther and I sing duets, and the children all sing, too. Some of our happiest times have been these church programs.

All this I sit and remember as I am feeling sorry for myself because Luther has to leave tomorrow to be gone for a week. Campfires of hoboes at night along the lonely river, or trucks that prowl to steal our melons can make the farm a different place by dark. I still don't relish being alone here, although it won't be like one other time years ago when I put the three youngsters and myself in one bed, lying crosswise. I brought Katchem, the dog, inside and feared nothing with him near. But the next morning I found he had chewed up a pair of leather mittens and an overshoe. No more dog inside.

If I can see each day as one more step toward a goal, it is easier than if I look ahead at an endless chain of days filled always with the same monotonous tasks. So I remind myself that just as each child is different from every other, so is each day in some ways different from every other day.

Animals are different, too, with their own individualities. I had a young rooster that crowed one whole day in a high falsetto voice, "What's going to happen now? What's going to happen now?" His voice must have been changing; I've not heard him crow like that since.

We have spoiled our cat, Madam Queen. We got her as a kitten ten years ago. She sleeps in the rocking chair. At meal times, she parks by Luther's chair, and if food is not forthcoming, she plants her forepaws on his thigh and sometimes sinks her claws in deep. That gets her food and a sharp reprimand. Luther says the Coolidges feed their dog at the table. So if it's all right for the White House, it's all right for him to feed Madam Queen, too.

Madam Queen is considered cute, clever, and wise by the rest of us. We used to mark on the calendar how may rats she killed. We knew when we found their skins. Then she became so surfeited she ate only the heads; finally she left them whole and killed for the sport of it. Perhaps she thinks we yet lack a few stages of reaching civilization, and that worries me a little -- too little.

You always believed in physical fitness. You took deep breathing exercises every morning after breakfast was on the stove. So you might be interested in the new "setting up exercises:" you throw a hundred pennies all over the room and pick them up one by one. I would need to throw only fifty, and pick up after my two boys after they've gone to school every morning.

At any rate, there's no need for me to pick up pennies. I picked up potatoes Saturday; all of us did. Our potatoes had every requisite for good growth and yield because they were made before the August heat set in. But the seed was poor; all the yield we got from one bushel of seed was one bushel of potatoes. The yield should have been fourteen. Most of our digging was in vain. In the end, we were happy just to get our seed back. Something ought to be done about potato seed that has been sold to the farmer the last few years.

I know you miss the Nebraska climate, Mother, though you don't realize it. In your letters, occasionally you say, "Oh, how beautifully the sun shines today." Out here the sun shines all the time. I always miss the sun on a cloudy day, which is seldom. Some day, with soil conservation in full swing, we won't have the dust with our strong winds, and they will just be high winds, bracing and invigorating. I know it will be hard on the complexion, but I'll not complain.

You were carrying a tintype of Dad in his late twenties around with you the last time you were out here, and showing him proudly to all and sundry. It takes years of living with a man to learn how to get along with him smoothly. You lived with one man all your married life, and carried his tintype picture in your purse after he had gone on. And so will I live with one man, till death do us part. We do fight, fight for the zest of it, I think (even the children walk out on us), and still we are madly in love with each other. I should change "madly" - "madly" is for honeymooners, I suppose.

You and I have children because we wanted to. But it will be so women will have to be bribed by the government to increase, the cost is so high. The baby crop is falling off in the cities. A neighbor of mine who came from St. Joseph said doctors charged forty dollars for confinement, and some seventy-five dollars. Of course they brought nurses with them. Ours cost twenty dollars, and one even fifteen dollars. They did nurses' and doctors' duty both. God bless the good doctors. No wonder they die in the prime of life. We have lost two doctors we were attached to, and another lost his health and thereby his practice.

I know a woman who lost her life trying to dispense with the services of a doctor during confinement. She had had several healthy children, and usually had an easy time of confinement. But she had her first hemorrhage with this one, and before a doctor could get there, it was too late for both mother and babe. Tragic, yes. We cannot afford to lose one single mother or child. I suppose we will soon be making hectic plans like Germany and Italy to build up a dwindling population. The way is to make confinement safer and cheaper - right now.

The flippant 20's! I even bought bread. We never butchered; we bought doughnuts and cookies. It took me one and a half years to learn to bake good bread. We ate wheat out of the bin, ground, for eight months and liked it. We use feed sacks for sheets. No, Mother, not gunny sacks -- feed sacks like flour sacks. I used to wear underwear you'd made out of flour sacks. I don't remember any sheets like these, though.

I do love all my sister farmers with their red "dishwater hands." I wish I were a fairy who could give them every one electricity in their homes, or a lot more leisure, or at the very least, great huge Crisco cans of good cold cream. I admire them.

Dust storms! Man has made a terrible mistake plowing up virgin pasture and planting cultivated crops. Dry weather comes, and all the soil blows away. Jane says she will always remember her first dust storm:

"We were at school, and somebody said, 'A terrible black cloud is coming!' We didn't know what it was or what to do. The teacher didn't know what to do, either. She sent us home. The sun was covered. The dust was hitting our faces. We couldn't talk, it was settling in everything we wore. When we got home, we found it piling up on the floor. It sifted in through doors and windows, and we could hardly breathe. People -- even little babies -- were dying, from dust getting into their lungs. I can still smell it right now. That smell will never leave me."

Dust. Wind. Snow. Rain. We watch for them all. The smoke from the cement plant is our barometer like the Mountains Catskill were to the Dutch housewives in "Rip Van Winkle." If the smoke rises straight up, it means fair weather; if it rises, then sinks toward the ground, we know rain or bad weather is on the way...

I don't believe you were ever bothered much by beetles like we have this summer. There are red ones, black ones, striped, and a beautiful russet brown. Beetles are a new pest that seems to have emerged with dictators and other modern evils. I learned two things not to do to get rid of them: spray with coal oil (kills the plant), dust with lime (injures the plant and is ineffective). The other season we had merely to stamp the foot and make terrible Apache yells to get them to scamper out of the patch and never come back.

But there were too many this summer. Their numbers made them bold. They migrated from the potato patch on to the tomatoes. They began by eating the tomato leaves, but later they actually skinned the tomatoes and left them hanging nude on the vines. The beetles got the major part of the tomato crop. The only known way to kill beetles without injuring the plant is to chase them down with a club and smash them. (That might discourage dictators, too, yes?)

Jane really did get to college this year. We began planning it eight months ago. At times, it looked to be an impossible feat to accomplish. One night this summer, as I was just about to fall asleep, Betty Lou piped up from the adjoining bedroom, "Mama, do you know how I remember always to say my prayers now? I hear Jane whispering hers every night." I smiled to myself. I knew the theme of Jane's prayers was getting to go on to school.

We began by writing for school catalogs from most of the universities in the state, always inquiring about chances for a student working for room and board. The state-supported schools were frank in saying they advised against a student working, and it finally simmered down to a choice between two small church colleges. About two weeks before school began, the Dean of Women at Wesleyan sent her the names of four women to whom she could apply to work for room and board.

One woman answered her application at once, but she was ten blocks from the campus, which I think is too far for a student working. Then we got a card from a professor at Hastings, saying they needed a girl to work the week before school, and that she could look for work while there. So we threw her things together; Luther took her to catch the early morning bus for the professor's house. The next day we got a letter from another woman at Alma College who offered her a place in her home, just a block from the campus.

We began writing to Jane that perhaps she ought to take the job in hand in place of two in the bush. She wrote back that she could work for the faculty members for room and board for the year. In her next letter, she was elated and joyous; she had been to a formal, served punch in the corner, and said she met the nicest young man.

Her third letter was dejected. She talked of coming home Thanksgiving, ten weeks away. She had been to a party and couldn't dance, so was a wall flower. Life can be so tragic at seventeen! Things must be better now; she hardly writes at all. I will send her a wire or phone call collect. That's the way

I'll do all of my four when they get away. If I can afford it, I'll send stamps and a questionnaire.

I don't know, but I'm pretty sure I've taken my last car trip; I'm going by train after this. I don't like the noise and din of cities. Most of it is made by cars. Or I've been away from it so long I'm alien to it. When Pearl and I came to see you last spring in Michigan, Mother, crossing streets was a nightmare. The cars lined up seemed like demons, held in leash only by a red light.

I got so I shut my eyes, and held on to Pearl's arm. I told myself that she would suffer mentally more than I would physically if she let me get run over. When I got home and got word of Uncle Frank's being struck and killed by an auto in the street, I fairly shuddered and was grateful to be home all in one piece again.

Oh, for the good old days when we guarded our credit at the bank religiously with our lives, and could pay the interest if we couldn't pay the note when it came due. When you go to a banker for a loan, you are shown into a private cubicle, but not so in a resettlement office. There are others at your elbow, and you feel like you bare your soul, and you catch yourself unashamedly listening to the personal and private affairs of others. Two of the welfare people come from families in slim circumstances, as did the office steno. These girls are personal and understanding. For the others, you have to fit a pattern instead of making a pattern fit you. Advising, the banker does expertly, smoking an endless chain of cigarettes, while trying to unravel the knotty problems of clients.

But the dole is bitter fruit to partake of. It disrupts that friendly neighborly feeling in a community. The non-partakers watch you zealously to find out in what ways you mis-spend it: changes of cars, picture shows, beer consumption. Many of them have been trying to keep their heads above water, and many are taxpayers who feel they are paying additional taxes to take care of the dole load.

The summons said, "bring your wife with you." We went. We wives never read a line, signed a paper, or did anything but stand around uncomfortably in the heat, and wonder why we came or were sent for. We went home, disgruntled that they could take our day's time and discomfort so lightly. No official said our coming was a mistake, or that they were sorry for the inconvenience they had caused us. Perhaps they wanted to see how we were standing the hot weather.

We are not wearing stripes, but we feel them. We have been in three bank failures. Luther used to boast that in all the years he had borrowed money, he never had given a chattel mortgage, a lien on assets, other than real estate. That was before our resettlement. But now he will never have the face to say that again, because we have plastered everything so thoroughly that we would be lucky to get out with our shirts if they were to foreclose and use all their inherent powers and advantages.

We are warned to read all the little fine print in the contracts of fly-by-night salesmen, but one had better read Uncle Sam's contracts too. Our load is terribly top heavy; over half of it went for feed. We've had two crop failures, and with another one, it will surely topple over. Now we wish we had gone along unhelped. Anyone who has had Uncle Sam for a banker once will not want him again, I warrant you.

Would any banker but Uncle Sam summon you nineteen miles on a blistering hot day and offer you neither a chair nor a fan? Would any banker but Uncle Sam not express regret that you were summoned by mistake - and leave you wondering whether it was a mistake?

Farm people are the most mulish people on earth. We are grateful to dairy men for resisting, showing good old American independence. John L. Lewis cast a covetous eye on the large farm population, thought he could perhaps gather them under his protective wing. He would start with dairy men. What did the dairy men do? They would have none of him; they shied away from him as though he were leprous. They even lost money in order to resist him. No, farmers will never unionize.

But we do have a means right under our noses that would solve some of our difficulties: cooperatives. If the city will take to itself poultry raising by means of batteries in skyscrapers - chicken houses as big as the Empire State Building - we will start factories and cooperatives out here, and work for wages in them. For several years, we haven't made poultry pay. We have joined an R.E.A. cooperative. I hope that a taste of its success will lead to other cooperatives. They are a weapon for both buying and selling. We take others' prices, their weights, and because our produce is perishable, we must go along with them. With cooperatives, we could be more financially independent than any AAA, FSA, etc., etc., has ever made us.

Luther and I were married on the Thanksgiving after Armistice Day, 1918. The price of farm produce the year following was highly satisfactory, but building material was correspondingly high, so we planned to build a small shelter then and build a house when we could better afford it. It was a little three room place, which was not a house but was a home. The back of the house rested in the bank at the top of the river bottomland, the front, on posts driven in the ground.

As it turned out, we lived in those three rooms till all of my family was here. I did have a dream house in mind. The plans, in fact, were so vivid in my mind that I sent them in to the "Country Gentleman," and the magazine used them in a story. The author used quotations from my letters. My neighbors recognized me in the magazine. Time went on and the depression loomed. We were glad to have any kind of shelter with enough to stave off hunger. Then came repeated droughts, but I still had hopes.

"The Country Gentleman" asked me to write when the house was built. It will never be built now. We do live in a different house, a four-room house the Red Cross helped us build. I like it very much, and it was the answer to a prayer, but it took a terrible upheaval to get it.

The Republican River had been high that June 5, in 1935. We had built a dike along the river side of our farm, which had kept out all minor floods. On Friday, the sixth of June, we walked up and down the dike measuring the rise and noting weak places in the dike. We filled in mole holes where water had begun to seep through.

At the lowest point in the dike on one of these tours, we discovered water beginning to slop over. We worked frantically with spade and shovel to build the dike a little higher. All worked, big and little. At about suppertime, we decided it was hopeless, so walked wearily back to the shack.

To move out, or not to move, was the problem. Luther said the water might go down before much came through, so we decided to wait till morning. Things looked no better in the morning, so Luther went up to Bostwick to the railroad station. There, he heard the telegraphed news from Red Cloud, about fifteen miles up the river. The message from the Red Cloud stationmaster said: "I see a wall of water coming... It's here... I'm gone..."

There was no longer a problem whether to move out. The only problem was whether we could move out fast enough.

Luther had bought a one-room office building in Bostwick, and moved it to our farm. It sat above our house on higher land, and all the neighbors and relatives who weren't busy moving out their own things, pitched in to help us move our belongings into this house. The "green house," we called it.

We moved the chickens up from the chicken house to the brooder house above. We moved harrows, discs, and cultivators from the rich bottomland; the irrigation system, we had to leave behind. We started to move in the afternoon. It was just before total darkness set in that the six-foot wall of water hit. The house and everything left on the bottomland went under.

The children stayed in Bostwick. They said the first thing they remembered in the morning was the roar of the water pouring down over the trees. The sound of water rushing over bent-down trees makes a loud and eerie rumble, like the sound of a great waterfall. It is a sound you never forget.

Whole trees floated by, with trunks two feet in diameter. Dead pigs went by; pigs, they say, try to swim, but cut their own throats with their front hooves. We saw cows and horses, debris of every possible description, parts of houses and barns. The bridge, strangely enough, stayed intact, though the water reached up to it. Big trees would hit the pilings, struggle and go under.

Jane told me once, long afterwards, how she had loved what happened right after the flood: "We got to go into Bostwick and live in the Kirkbride house. It had great huge rooms; it was fun - an interlude. I could sit on the stoop and hear the music from Joe Keifer's dance. I wanted to go so bad, but I knew you wouldn't let me." Dad knew beer was sold there.

Sunday morning, after finding that the water had reached its zenith, and was beginning to lower, we came back to the farm from Bostwick. We didn't lose any of our clothing or bedding in the flood, but we were already very low in that respect. Because of the long struggle through the depression, we had banked everything we could scrape together into putting in our corn crop and truck garden that year. Everything had been coming along nicely: onions, two hundred new strawberry plants, asparagus bed just put out the preceding fall, acres of potatoes planted, one hundred acres of corn just across the river to the South.

All of it went.

Jane remembers her dad after the flood, "just sitting and sitting, the longest time. He never once said how bad it was. It just seemed like he never gave up. He seemed to gain strength from something, just sitting there. I never could understand how he kept on."

That first Sunday, there must have been thousands who drove to the bridge and away again. Everyone I talked to braced me up, but one woman said, "Isn't it too bad," and began to pity me. My lower lip began to tremble, and I realized it truly was terrible. I hadn't had time to think about it before.

The one room of the green house was ten feet by fifteen feet. We put our bed there, and some of our furnishings were already there. We arranged things so that, although it was terribly crowded, there was a small cleared space in the center. We resurrected an old three-burner oil stove. I cleaned and worked with it, and finally got two burners to work. I was overjoyed. We had our hearth again. Home was here.

I felt indeed humbly grateful for a roof over our heads. I cooked something hot, and after dinner was cleared up, we all laid down and stretched across our bed area and slept for hours. As time went by, we began to get irritable and snappish with each other from living in too cramped quarters. But we never dreamed of changing. The children's prayer was: "Bless all the little orphans. Give the little Chinese something to eat. Dear God, help us to get a new house."

It was the Red Cross who brought this miracle to pass. They provided funds to build on to our one-room home: two bedrooms, a kitchen and a front porch. The CCC and WPA helped with the labor. I still smart at callous remarks sometimes made. The government did an injustice to workers by not enforcing a day's labor. The sluggards gave all the workers a bad name.

The Red Cross workers were wonderful. I remember a Mrs. Hill particularly. She had a soft Southern or Eastern drawl (I never could tell them apart), and I loved to hear her talk. She would butt into my line of talk without preamble, and yet apologized for the accidental popping of gum she was chewing. (Said she had never learned to chew gum right anyway.)

A local social worker left a check with me to buy groceries one day. It bore an insignia of the Federal Emergency Relief Administration. When Luther got home and saw it, he accused me of putting him on the F.E.R.A., welfare. We had one of the most heated quarrels we ever had. But it turned out that that was a stop-gap to the work of the Red Cross.

My heart swells with gratitude for the millions who give to the Red Cross. I felt them blessed in giving, as I felt blessed in receiving. I thought of the morning during the depression days that a woman came to my door. She asked me for a little flour, baking soda, corn meal. She said there were two of them in a covered wagon up at the bridge.

I gave her the things she asked for and then, as an afterthought, gave her six eggs. She was overjoyed with the eggs and exclaimed, "God bless you, honey." A warm tingly delicious feeling ran all through my being. I believed then and there that I had received God's blessing. I would like each Red Cross giver to feel that same sensation as I say and mean it, to each of them, "God bless you, honey."

The flood may have been the happiest summer and fall of my life, perhaps. I had more leisure. I'm by nature a lazy creature at housecleaning, mending; I like to cook and flower garden. It's surprising how little we can live well on, if by well, one means abundant food, shelter, and fuel. When we do get extra money, it is a nerve-wracking job to decide which of the things we want to get.

Jane told me once, after she was grown, a thing that meant a lot to me. "I never knew, mother, that we were poor."

If you look for beauty, you find it: insect life - wings and bodies; weeds - seed pods and flowers. Whose mind and hand fashioned these minute little creations? It must be harder to find God in cities, where man's eyes are continually upon man's handiwork. A farmer's are continually upon God's handiwork. There, man's achievements assume most importance; here, God's do.

Be still and know that I am God. I search for the God Jesus knew, Paul knew, my mother knows. I contact him nearer out in the fields under his dome, just sitting quietly relaxed, and noticing sounds I hear and things I see. And I let my thoughts go where they are led by these sounds and sights. Of a necessity, I am sitting where I can't see a road with cars racing madly in it. I can't see houses or barns. Only the river, tall trees, and open spaces. I hear silent things, see butterflies, clouds, dragonflies...

Some people have to have beauty pointed out to them, thus: "This thing is beautiful; it must be, everyone says it is." They can't find it for themselves. That must be why so many went mad over futurist art some years ago.

Mother, the word pictures you painted to me of the white birch trees in Michigan along a lake with moonlight I have never forgotten. I have three dead box elders growing up from the same base, which the woodpeckers have skinned almost completely. I can squint my eyes and they are birch. At night, by moonlight, I don't have to squint, and they are still birch.

Today, I drove the car over to the pasture to bring back Luther, who had walked over to drive some of the stock to pasture there. We walked over the pasture among the cattle looking for Sylvia, our strayed cow - the one with the broken, zigzag tail. We found her up on the highest point in the pasture. The view was wonderful to the north. Luther and I stood there a long time picking out landmarks we knew. To the east was the silver standpipe and terminal elevator in the town eleven miles away. The fields wore the usual harvest colors; from up here, you couldn't tell they had worn that look since midsummer.

The winding strips of green trees marked the course of the river. October's deep blue sky was overhead. It was the first time I have been on that hill.

Looking down, I discovered we were standing on what used to be the burial place for three or four bodies. You remember, one was that of a girl who died from the bite of a rattlesnake about forty years ago. The bodies have long since been removed to the cemetery at Bostwick.

There were matted beds of dwarf iris, and the stunted dead form of an evergreen tree. Luther said, "What a forlorn place for a grave." But I said, "What a gorgeous view to wake up to." And I made a vow to stand on that same spot after frost had turned the trees to vivid yellows and orange.

I live all year for October, and here it is. I grope for words to tell the beauty in common place things. I find so many people could enjoy a beautiful autumn if they didn't keep peering ahead into the hazardous winter. I believe such people should enjoy that hazardous winter more because they are peering ahead into the spring.

I often wonder if the autumn season of the year does not symbolize the autumn of life. It should be beautiful and gracious, too, but those people who spend fall grumbling about winter, spend their autumn in life complaining about infirmities, aches and discrepancies of their physical handicaps. They fail to realize that their mental and spiritual faculties are still intact, and they should be ready for enjoyment of a full life of experiences.

Luther, Junior, was born July 6, 1932. We called him - lightly - our "depression baby." We never imagined that he felt a stigma was attached to that expression until one day he became very angry at his older brother. He searched for words to express the ultimate exasperation. He exploded: "You - you depression baby, you!"

Warren K. earned Luther Junior's everlasting dislike by calling his horse, Tom, a "plug." Luther Junior told him he didn't know horseflesh. How he loves Tom. He paid hard-earned cash for a curry-brush and comb for Old Tom. I'm going to use them on Luther Junior.

We had an old harrow, a real find for the scrap iron drive - but one end of it was left deeply imbedded in the ground. So we left it for later evacuation. Luther Junior, at eleven, was impatient. After the rest of us were out of sight, he bridled Old Tom, the horse. He tied one end of a long rope through the harrow sticking out of the ground; the other end, he tied securely around his own waist. Mounting Old Tom, he gave a sharp kick to Old Tom's ribs. Tom was off at a gallop. The harrow remained stationary. So did Luther Junior - on the ground.

One cold day in the winter, I kidded Luther Junior about being cold. Where was his Indian blood he pretended so much? He jerked off his coat, two shirts, tied his overalls around his waist, grabbed his milk bucket and shouted, "You'll see!" as he went out in the forty-five degree morning to milk. Now, at thirteen, Luther Junior is in a dither to get his legs tanned like his torso before Jane gets here for a visit from Boise, and teases him about his lily white legs. When he wears his red shorts, he has to put up with his Uncle John's comments. He'll probably decide to wear the shorts, and take to the bushes when Uncle John comes in sight.

Manners. The only way I can tell my talking penetrates to Luther Junior is when company comes. He chews with his lips closed and takes smaller bites, sits straight and doesn't take the biggest piece.

1944:

For crying out loud, is there anything so grueling as hot flashes when it's ninety degrees in the *shade*?

I'm fifty. A doctor says we begin to die at fifty. I look back and it begins to seem longer the way back than ahead. Now material things, possessions, and goals we used to have, have faded. We think more of comfort and our health.

I'm fifty. It's too late to make a big effort to get things I've had to do without. Everyday, the farm woman sees jobs on every side she looks that ought to be done but can't. Dear God, help her to choose first things to do first. Dogs to be dusted, wall cupboard to be cleaned and painted, kitcat to be varnished, brooder stoves and baby chick equipment to clean and put away, pickles, tomatoes, corn and beans to can, windows to wash, overalls to mend. I'd like to see the farm woman who keeps everything up. Is it possible?

A friend said she heard I dyed my hair. I laughed and was noncommittal. I felt flattered that people would think me fastidious enough to take the trouble to dye my hair. My husband doesn't feel that way; he says I shouldn't like people to think that. The fine point is knowing when to be obtuse, and when not to be. I confess it escapes me most of the time.

They say catnaps are a sign of age. But I wake fully refreshed afterwards. Just observe dogs and cats napping; humans should follow suit.

More and more, as it becomes harder to get material possessions, our children become an increased treasure. Perhaps when they all get to the age of making their own way, conditions will be different in the world. I hope so. I've seen countless high school graduates, at first bewildered, then alarmed, finally despondent over not being able to work.

The more you give of yourself to your children, the more you get back from them. Money, shelter, and clothes are not enough. Some parents make the parental house too soft a cushion. The fledglings are reluctant to try their wings. A farm home is not as apt to do this as is a small town. There is too much work to do. We get the young birds through high school; after that, they must get themselves through at least two years of college, either by working, or borrowing, or both.

The third bird, Betty, is just beginning. The oldest girl, Jane, is now in Boise, Idaho, working for United Air Lines. Betty has gone to Boise, too, and Jane had money placed on deposit for her. Betty abused the credit, but had to pay it back. She was allowing her roommate to charge grocery bills, even some items like candy bars.

David, in the Navy now, is dispirited because he is twenty, and no money saved; he could have two thousand dollars in the bank if he had not gone to college for two years in Michigan. Was his college worth it? "College can teach me to think, but so can living and reading..."

We elders are tempted to try to help our young learn from our experience. It seldom works: my brother, John, was helping Luther Junior harness horses one zero morning. John told him that if he touched his tongue to the metal on the bridle, it would take the skin right off his tongue. Luther promptly touched his tongue to the bridle. It did.

Luther Junior, after unloading cobs in the east brooder house, went down to the bridge to turn around. Instead of taking the trouble to open the gate, he pulled just a little north in order to back on the road again, and head west. But that little distance was just a little too far. The frost was out, and the ground was spongy for a depth of eighteen inches. Luther Senior came storming into the house: "I told that boy not to get off the road!"

This was sound advice, Luther Senior having got stuck two times that afternoon in the road. I put on my boots and went down to see if I could give some pertinent suggestions. Luther Junior was indeed stuck: all four wheels were down to their hubs. He was using the jack against the hub rim to raise each wheel. I held a long board for him to rest the jack on.

Luther Senior joined us: "This car will be right here in the mud this time tomorrow."

"Do you want to bet on it?"

"I'd bet ten dollars on it if I was a betting man." (I offered to hold their bets, but neither of them had ten dollars to their name.)

Luther Junior began the craziest operations I had ever seen. He began to rock the car first. Front wheels went up on long boards, and then came back against the back wheels. He got out and spaded mud from behind the back wheels. He got in and rocked again. He would ask, "Dad, do you think I'll get out?"

"No, but I hope you do."

Another rock. "Dad, am I going to get out?" No answer. On the next rock - finally - he was out.

Guidance - Freedom: a difficult balance. If we guide children in food and dress habits, why shouldn't we also in religion until they are ready to take over for themselves? All born little liars have to be taught to love the truth.

The Old Testament was a stumbling block to me in my youth. Somehow, I had picked up the idea that all the Old Testament characters were holy men perfect in the sight of God, and I used to secretly scoff at them for their shortcomings. But I wouldn't have dared to take my doubts to my mother or my Sunday School teacher, for fear of being branded an unbeliever.

In our early marriage days, at first I went to Sunday School because it was necessary in the country to take small children. My husband went, too. I remember Jane sitting in her little chair by the preacher. After each child came, I quit, and wouldn't have started again were it not for the prodding two women gave me.

After I returned each time, I realized I had been missing something that I unconsciously needed. I would find an answer to a perplexing problem. The children were better. Once when I couldn't find words to explain something to them, there it was in the Sunday School lesson by Luccock.

Children belong to God first, and then to their parents. Always, when I have kept that truth in mind, I have been a better parent. I have been more patient, understanding.

There are some advantages to War Time: the evenings are longer and more enjoyable and I can work with yard flowers. Our mid-day meal, dinner, is over before the hottest part of the day. Although it's a hustle, it's nice to be back from Sunday School before the hottest part of the day. There is a disadvantage to the family in winter when the farmer (if ever) can relax; he must rise at five o'clock central time to get children off to school, or earlier, to catch a bus that goes before daylight.

I am amazed by the change radio has made in people like me. Hank Schultz, in the doctor's office, was giving his opinion on Russia, with a complete layout. At Kensington Women's Club, there's a lack of gossip; the discussion around the quilt is of current topics.

Mussolini's wife told reporters that she wished now she and her husband had immigrated to America as they had planned when they were first married. If they had, would he be one of our militant labor leaders now?

We must make some accommodations. For example, sugar is scarce: use two saccharine tablets and one third cup syrup for lemonade; syrup for breakfast food; eat sweet baked rolls for dessert. Our Navy cadet sends his wash home, two sheets in a laundry case; he has to wait five weeks for laundry there.

July, 1945

Am I a chastened woman! Last spring, I asked the three fledglings who had left the parental nest to entreat divine daily guidance and help, daily, for our work here at home so that we might raise a bumper crop to lift the mortgage, or at least lighten it perceptibly. They must have cooperated, for never did our spring work progress so easily or well. The three of us got along with very little outside help.

On July 16, we had ten thousand beautiful cabbages just ready to begin marketing at five cents per pound. Two thousand tomato plants each with its share of fruit to ripen. Cantaloupe vines were spreading their green quilt over the bare ground. Sweet corn was in the tassel stage. Luther and Luther Junior had done it practically alone; hours of my time were taken up with chickens and housework. I had a fine flock of three pullets and as many roosters coming on.

But on the afternoon of July 16 came the deluge. It began raining late in the afternoon, just a continuous pouring. I picked up a magazine and began to read to take my mind off of that pounding rain on the roof.

Our garden plot surrounded by a dike is on bottomland below the house, with the river on one side. An ordinary rain leaves nothing but improvement in its wake, a too heavy rain swells the runoff water above us into a creek, and that's what happened this time. Five inches fell in three hours. The river rose, and went over the dike on the other side. We not only lost the cabbage, we had to smell them when the wind was in the Southwest.

We can't stop the hens from dying, so we'll cart them off to market. They'll bring $1 per head. We've sold $104 worth of fryers. We can pay a fuel bill of $18, $10 for car repair, and put $100 in the bank to feed the pullets. We'll keep 56 hens, but have lost two of them, so we may have to sell the hens, too. It is a good thing we have the pullets to turn our hopes to. Eggs are 43cents top grade now.

I think we will have some sweet corn to market, as the water didn't hurt it too much. We are eating tomatoes; some are beginning to come back. Dad said he would plant rye on the bare ground. John has a bumper wheat crop in Kansas. Some wheat on his land made 50 bushels and some 35. His share will be $2600.

Of course, income tax will cut it all down.

The mosquitoes are AWFUL here.

The war with Japan is going great guns. I wouldn't be surprised to have it end almost any time.

I was wrong to ask the children to pay for our material gain. It is of the least importance. I'm going to quote from today's Sunday School lesson: "Material blessing is not the blessing of the Christian life. God does not make us rich, or preserve us from all ill. God's part is to love us as His children, to give us strength to meet whatever comes to us. To help us attain the abundant life of the spirit, and to enter life eternal some day. Our part: to make the things that matter most with God matter most to us."

After a headache of three days duration, the world again seems rosy; life is good.

There is a lesson for us in the way nature comes back after a flood. The cantaloupes, stunned, put out new shoots and start blooming immediately to be sure and make seed fruit before fall. Potato vines appear dead; little leaves begin to sprout over branches. Tomatoes start out with only one leaf. The cabbage and sweet corn are still unknown. Each, in its own way, seeking - finding - the miraculous rhythm of the universe.

The shock of our loss has disappeared, and I feel very strongly a guiding hand behind it all. Everything will turn out all right.

Jane said once, "It seemed there's always been a flood every two or three years. I couldn't see how my dad could keep on planting that stuff over and over. And over and over, it would flood. But every time it flooded, it would leave a thick silt. Dad got all the good topsoil, I think, from every other upstream farm in the country on our little farm. He grew tremendous vegetables in a good year."

And David asked Dad once, "Why do you stay?" "Because it's home," Dad answered.

I first heard about Jane's romance on July 29: She wrote, "I've been going out with a soldier from Los Angeles. He has a nice car and really takes me to nice places. But nothing special."

August 18: "I'm positive this is it this time. I'm in love again. His name is Howard. He has asked me to go steady with him."

August 20: "I'm going to get married in a month to Howard. We are so much in love. I never knew it could be like this."

It's true we live our life in our children. I visualize Jane; every morning she wakes up with this feeling, "Where am I? Why do I have this elated feeling? Oh, yes, I'm to be married Saturday!"

Now I wake up every morning with this glowing inside me and in turn ask, "Where am I? Why do I have this elated feeling? Oh, yes, Jane's to be married Saturday!" It's true, sometimes doubts assail me; how can she be sure he is *the* man on such short acquaintance?

One young rooster here took up his abode in the hen house after we sold off all the old roosters. When

I turn them out, he comes out of a different pen every morning. He chases back any other young males that dare to saunter down from the brooder house. He takes a vicious peck at my ankles when my back is turned.

How like humans.

Hitler developed into a big bully because we did not interfere; he thought we were afraid of him, until in our slow-burning wrath, we had him cowering in tunnels under Berlin. I keep thinking, why did we let an earlier big bully, Mussolini, shower gas bombs on the helpless Ethiopians and brag about it? Now, as a result of all our bungling of the Golden Rule, we find ourselves using the atomic bomb. Of course it is wicked to use it. For being wicked in not helping the Ethiopians, we have to be wicked again to bring peace once more to the world.

Black oilcloth mourning will change when Japan gives up. These days, we are watching war with one eye, and peace with the other. Russia wants vengeance on conquered countries, including Japan. We want only justice. The more MacArthur digs below the surface, we find in Japan that which may be found in any country: the common mass of people who pay the terrible cost of war. Vengeance on them would not give the satisfaction that justice would. Nor would vengeance yield the ultimate good to all mankind that justice administered to our archenemy will.

Good Will: this spirit is possible; when it finds expression, it is immensely powerful. Think of unexpected things to do for people - unlooked for things that say convincingly that we have been thinking of them. Acts of good will are desperately needed in our country today, acts that reach across fences separating one religion from another, one race from another - "racial tension and religious antagonism." We can treat people as individuals on their own personal merit.

Boys who are coming back, bless their hearts, have become articulate. Travel has broadened their outlook. They have opinions of their own - and no longer hesitate to express them to men ten years and more their senior.

A cholera-like disease on our farm along with the flood prevented us from attending Jane's wedding on September 1 in Boise. When Jane told Betty she was getting married, tears came into Betty's eyes as she hugged her sister. Tears of relief, I know -- Betty was worrying, afraid Jane wouldn't get a man. Jane was the hoary age of twenty-five.

For the first time in thirty years, I have leisure time. That's the reason I am piecing together this little mosaic of thoughts and memories. I take my hands out of dishwater, dry them, to jot down an idea before it is lost, then I go back to dishwashing. I used to use chicken grease on my hands in the depression. I'm not proud, but not ashamed.

I like a man who can do things with his hands: chop wood and have the ax hit where he says. I believe the two thrive together, mental and manual labor.

I am still a dot-dash housekeeper: a dot here and a dash there.

Luther asked me to go out with him to hunt up a little wood. The day is beautiful, and I am tempted to go with him but I stamp my foot and say, "The very idea! I haven't done breakfast dishes or gotten the separator washed yet." So I thrust Satan behind me and dig in to finish my work as fast as I can, so I can get out with Luther to where I love to be. He knows, and I know, that by force of will power, I am putting behind me the impulse of grabbing my jacket and old black felt and slamming the door on the unwashed dishes behind me.

Ironing. Thin cool ruffles round the neck, loops on each sleeve, and triple rows beneath each pocket.

White shirts.

Oh, how I dislike ironing white shirts. If I were a crying woman, I would have shed pints of tears over my ironing board. Whoever invented the fad of white shirts? If I were a betting woman, I would bet ten to one it wasn't a woman.

Are there safety pins on Mars? My guess would be yes.

There's one spot on Sunday noon radio that I insist on. It is Sammy Kaye's orchestra. I'm usually doing the dinner dishes. Really, I don't know what task I'm doing while I'm listening. Dad wants to know how I can stand such drooling.

I've had poor luck with radio recipes, so I get new recipes from two superb cooks in the neighborhood: sisters-in-law, one German descent, the other, Bohemian. One told me how to make good piecrusts. So often I ask what's new in cooking; they always tell me never to leave out ingredients. I'd give my eye teeth (if I had any) to cook like they do.

The way to a man's heart is pie: apple, lemon, grape or custard, chocolate cream or apricot. Custard pie is my husband's favorite. I've tried all ideas, and had partial success with all, but never the perfect custard pie: brush the crust with fat and set in the refrigerator - partially bake and pour in the liquid - brush the crust with egg white - scald milk before mixing with the egg.

I can dream for hours of the advantages that could be mine by making the perfect custard pie.

A long distance view out your kitchen window is good for your eyes. You watch for the mailman or the mister to come up the road. The change in eye focus from short to long distance strengthens the eye, doctors say.

Do our city sisters watch for the mailman? Is the coming of the mailman such a highlight in each day for our city sisters as it is for us? If he goes by at noon and doesn't leave the letter I'm yearning for, I am terribly let down for a few hours, and then I rally and begin to hope for one for sure on the morrow.

Luther raises fancy chickens, prize winning White Leghorns. We dug out a cellar. We took big timbers from the rebuilding of the bridge, and put them across, and covered them with dirt. In that cellar are the incubators.

Jane used to pity me, she told me once. "You used to have to go down night and morning and turn those eggs. All those eggs. One at a time. Next day, the same thing all over, turn the eggs until those little chickens were hatched. I hated to see you do it. I was too little to help. I remember thinking, 'what a big job.' I thought you were spending all your time turning eggs."

I confess, I thought so, too. Raising chickens is the dirtiest work on a farm. From her shoes to her hair, a woman gets polluted in chicken and brooder houses. I get down and crawl around the brooder for the first weeks, placing chicks evenly around the hover at night.

A woman puts so much in chickens. I hate chicken thieves. Even cats. Our cat eats eggs every day; she eats three if she can get them. She and I have a game. I try to beat her to the nests. I have to gather four or five times a day if I want to be ahead of her.

How I would like a brooder house of my own to try out some of the ideas I have gathered through thirty years of chicken raising. Of course, the new city-style mass production may take over poultry raising, but we would still keep a cock to crow, and a few hens and chicks for our own use.

I even venture to tell Luther how to garden. I got very excited last winter after reading "Plowman's Folly," and talked about it for a couple of months until, in desperation, Luther put out tomato plants the "Folly" way, in cabbage rows: namely, tamp ground to facilitate capillary attraction, lay a tomato plant down, and cover it with dirt, firmed down. The tomatoes raised their heads, and are producing now.

I wonder, will DDT used around brooder houses make it possible for the farmer to utilize one of his best food byproducts for chickens? Milk. Sour milk is good for so many intestinal disorders in chicks. Up to now, the big drawback to using milk was flies, which cause tapeworms in chickens.

And will we someday be able to sit on our lawns and eat without being pestered by flies and mosquitoes, thanks to DDT, as well?

Nature has some of its own remedies. I freed a housed ladybug. Once I gave a neighbor lettuce, and said she was welcome to the lettuce, but please pick off the ladybugs and leave them in the garden. She looked at me in amazement, and said the ladybugs were eating her garden up. I explained that they were after the lice, which were eating her garden up.

I love country life! With all my five senses:

Taste - sweet corn, tomatoes, fried chicken, cold milk

Smells -ozone, new cut alfalfa, wild grapes, sweet horse alfalfa in bloom after a shower, my volunteer petunia bed

Touch - a furry kitten

Sight - sunset, the blue sky lying flat on my back, the firmament of stars, yellow wheat next to a July corn field

Hearing - kingbirds, dawn meadow larks, cardinals, robins, popping of corn in the big iron skillet, the breeze through the cottonwoods, the mating call of the raccoon, country women chatting.

All this, and heaven, too. A great day is coming: electricity, with deep freeze, iron, lights, dishwasher, mixer, television.

I want just one piece of equipment at a time: first, lights - then an iron - then a vacuum cleaner.

When a group of farm women gets together, the freezer-locker holds the spot of discussion. Even city women speak longingly. We will have all the advantages of city life, and none of its disadvantages, and the bigger drawbacks of living in the country will fast disappear.

Every man, his vine and fig tree. After all, our Creator meant man to be thus. Electricity: the thrill and joy of it! In the post war days, the meticulous housekeeper will not know what to do with the time saved in housekeeping.

I will.

PHOTOGRAPHS

Sod and limestone home in Jewell County, Kansas, with 10 of the 12 Morgan children: Left to right, Clara, John, Harvey, Leonidas, Howard, Eva, Olive, Mary Elizabeth, Kathryn, Jane, Edna, Lena. Ruth and Pearl were born after the family moved across the border to Bostwick, Nebraska

Leonidas Taylor Morgan, Mary Elizabeth Harvey Morgan

Grandmother Harvey, "the feisty little lady who came from Ireland at age 3"

The Morgan family, left to right: Leonidas, Mary, Eva, John, Harvey, Olive, Kathryn, Jane, Edna, Pearl, Ruth, Lena and Howard. (Missing: Clara)

The Bostwick Hotel/boardinghouse

Kate, Lena, Pearl, Ruth, Eva and Edna: "The party couldn't get in full swing...till the Morgan girls were there."

The same 6 "Morgan girls" in 1961: Ruth, Eva, Edna, Lena, Kate and Pearl.

1962: Ruth's son, David, leaning against Keifers' storefront; the dances were held in the floor above. (Note 1930's type gasoline pump on right side of photo).

1972 - Side view of the same store, with Ruth and grandchildren in front of where an outside stairway once led to the dances.

Chautauqua program, describing Ruth's part in setting up children's activities

Ruth and Luther E. Smith, when they first met each other at Chautauqua

Ruth and Luther E. Smith as young people

Mr. and Mrs. L. T. Morgan
announce the marriage of their
daughter
Ruth
to
Mr. L. Edward Smith
on Thursday, November the twenty-eighth
nineteen hundred eighteen
Superior, Nebraska

*Their 1918
wedding
announcement*

Late 1920's: Ruth with Jane, David and Betty (on Ruth's lap)

Luther with the three children

Luther Junior, who was born in 1932

Luther Junior, and David

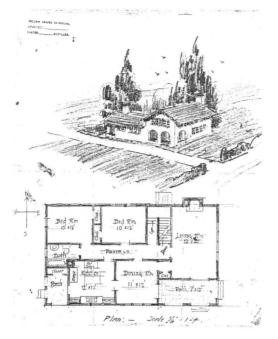

Architect's drawing of Ruth's dream house, published in "The Country Gentleman." "The neighbors recognized me in the magazine."

Letter from architect.

MEMBER

AUTHORS' LEAGUE OF AMERICA
AMERICAN SOCIETY OF AGRICULTURAL ENGINEERS
AMERICAN INSTITUTE OF ARCHITECTS
NATIONAL FIRE PROTECTION ASSOCIATION

WILLIAM DRAPER BRINCKLOE
"EDGEMAR"
EASTON, MARYLAND

May 30, 1928.

Mrs. Luther E. Smith
Bostwick, Nebraska.

Dear Mrs. Smith:

It's mighty nice to get such an appreciative letter from you! The house was an interesting one to plan; - just a bit out of the ordinary.

Your letters were very clear; they told me exactly what I wanted to know. Moreover, they were human;- they sounded as if you were talking to me, not just writing! So, I have copied them, very nearly word for word, in my article describing the house; but I haven't given your address, of course. Just when this article will appear, I don't know; - perhaps not for some time.

Please be sure and write me, when the house is actually built.

Very sincerely,

WDB:W

The Red Cloud Railroad station, and a the telegraph from which the message was probably sent to warn Bostwick: "I see a wall of water coming. I'm gone."

A general photo of the Republican River area, showing the extent of flood damage in the 1935 flood

After the 1935 Republican River flood: the back of their "little 3-room place," which rested on the river bank

*The barn, just beyond
the house, demolished
in the flood*

*Bridge above the Smiths' farm at flood stage, probably about
1938. The bridge survived the '35 flood, but, already weakened,
the later flood damaged it enough so that it had to be replaced
by the one shown in a 1985 photo. The bridge had 3 spans,
which leads to the estimate that the river when full at this point
would have been 300 or more feet across.*

1935/36: the "new 4 room house the Red Cross helped us build."

Photo of the new house in later years, 1975.

Dear mother

In between the lines of your last letter I can detect the loneliness that you feel during the day while the girls are working at their jobs. Just this week I find myself at a loss during the middle hours of the day too. The youngest of your 27 grandchildren started to school Monday! and does he love it! It seems so odd. I straighten up the house in the morning and it stays that way till about 4:30 P.M. I lay the scissors down and when I look for them again, there they are. But Oh, it is so quiet! The first day I caught myself singing or whistling at intervals all day to break up that strange continuity of stillness...

Have you tried the new "setting up exercise". Jumping out of bed, throwing a hundred pennies broadcast over the room then stooping to pick each one up by itself? I would need to throw only fifty and "pick up" after my two sons have left for school.

You couldn't guess what I'm doing today. I've taken it upon myself to keep the cows out of the tomatoe patch. Dan wanted to turn them in the truck patch to clean up some good pasture there. But I objected because I had pepper plants with fruit to ripen and a few

Ruth's original writing, indicating how she jotted things down as she thought of them, on whatever was handy at the moment

*1942 photos of family:
Above, Luther, Jr.,
Jane, David, Betty.
Left, Luther, Ruth.*

Mr. and Mrs. Luther Smith of Bostwick, Nebraska, and Mr. Dayle Free, Poultry Specialist at the University of Nebraska, receiving an air-borne shipment of breeding stock from the J. A. Taison White Leghorn farm of Corvallis, Oregon. These chicks are from five generation U. S. R. O. P. mating. The chicks have a guaranteed double pedigree of 300 egg production and are actually rated 300 to 358. The University will use some of this stock f orpoultry improvement work. The Smiths think buttermilk helps keep birds in tip top health and laying condition.

Luther E. Smith with some of his HANSEN White Leghorns. He has been raising this particular strain for the past 10 years. Each year cockerels valued at $25.00 each are purchased for continuous improvement of the flock. Hens are trap nested. All hens have a record of more than 300 eggs per year and in some cases have a record as high as 354 eggs per year. Many days during the fall the production record is 100%. The eggs are large, weighing 26 ounces per dozen. Hens weigh about 5 pounds. Mr. Smith lives one-half mile west of Bostwick.

Two clippings from "The Superior Express" about the Smiths' poultry business. (Note how people got "dressed up" to go to the airport).

Luther Junior teaching Ruth to drive the tractor

David, now a Navy carrier pilot

Jane, in Boise, Idaho, working for United Airlines

The family during the World War II years

Jane and Betty sightseeing at Hoover Dam, after Betty joined Jane in Boise

Jane brings new hubby, Howard Yeremian, home to meet the family, and Dave gets leave to join them

1950 cartoon by Vivian, on a visit, when the REA was about to bring the Smiths' electricity: "the thrill and joy of it!"

1950's visits

Grandpa Luther on back steps with granddaughter, Debi

David on the front porch with his mother, Ruth

Luther and Ruth with their family in 1959, beside the Bostwick Methodist Church (torn down sometime later)

Ruth and Luther

*1953: 35th
wedding
anniversary
portrait*

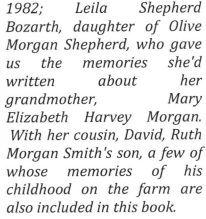

1982;   Leila   Shepherd Bozarth, daughter of Olive Morgan Shepherd, who gave us   the   memories   she'd written   about   her grandmother,   Mary Elizabeth Harvey Morgan. With her cousin, David, Ruth Morgan Smith's son, a few of whose   memories   of   his childhood on the farm are also included in this book.

Vivian and Debi Smith perform "Look Up at the Hawks" at the National Portrait Gallery

1987: view from the original site of the Kansas homestead, looking across the border to Nebraska, "where they moved, seeking better education for their children." Bostwick can be seen on the right, in the distance. Bob Keifer, grandson of the Keifers mentioned in Ruth's story, took the Smith family across the fields so they could visit the homestead site.

SUPPLEMENT

Leila Shepherd Bozarth, daughter of Ruth's 19 year older sister, Olive, wrote some of her own memories of her grandmother, Mary Elizabeth. They add a few vivid details to some of Ruth's family stories. In Leila's words:

It wasn't always easy to get Grandmother to talk of the past; she was always too busy with the present. Occasionally, I would find her in a reminiscent mood, and she would tell me of days when they lived in the sod house in Iowa.

It was not unusual then to have Indians come visiting. The men would talk to Grandfather in the barn, the squaws would file solemnly into the kitchen and watch Grandmother at work. When they went to leave, often one or two of the squaws would indicate a liking for something she saw – a spoon, pie, pan, cup – and Grandmother would urge the article as a gift. Better to give graciously than to incur enmity.

Visitors were few, but when they did come, it would be for a stay of several days, and their arrival would be the occasion for bringing out choice meat salted away, and favorite jars of preserves. The men would hunt during the day, the children enjoy new companions, and the women compare dress patterns, recipes, and prepare special food for the evening meal.

One story Grandmother told me was particularly poignant. She was expecting her fifth child, and preparations must be made. It had been a bad year financially, crops were poor, and money almost non-existent. Grandfather was going to town to trade the last of the potatoes for sugar and coffee, and Grandmother gave him a handful of carefully hoarded silver to buy flannelette. The newcomer would have to wear "hand-me-downs" mostly, but everybody was entitled to a few new pink and blue "pretties."

While Grandfather was gone, she got out her patterns, found some pink embroidery thread, and cleared a place on the table for cutting out. At the first sound of wagon wheels, she was out of the house in eager anticipation. Seizing the precious package, she tore off the wrapping, and then, to Grandfather's dismay, burst into tears! She had forgotten to designate pink or blue, and there before her were yards of dull, gray flannelette.

There was not a family in the neighborhood that had not, at some time, availed themselves of Grandmother's kindness, services, and generosity. As nurse and midwife, she was the recipient of thanks and gratitude, and sometimes a bushel of apples or a side of bacon. One family, who lived upon the hill back of the hotel, were what Grandmother called "shiftless." He was lazy, incompetent and irresponsible, incapable of holding down a job, but entirely capable of producing a offspring every year.

Mrs. ------- was a whining, complaining person, niggardly both in gifts and thanks for Grandmother's yearly midwife service. She was not much given to visiting or "neighboring," but there would come a day when Clara or Edna would spy her coming down the hill, baby on hip, a troop of scrawny, noisy children trailing behind her.

"Mother," Edna would call, "here comes Mrs. ------- with a jar of preserves. Another baby on the way!"

Apparently delinquency existed then as now, but Grandmother was determined that her children grow up to be responsibly, honest and honorable. She was waging a losing battle to keep her two sons from joining the older men in the poker game that flourished every Saturday night.

One night she could stand it no longer. Taking down her shawl, she marched across the street, through the general store, into the back room where the game was in progress. I have often imagined the astonished looks of the poker players as she reached over, swept the cards from the table, and threw them into the glowing, pot-bellied stove. Before anyone could speak, she marshaled her two sons in front of her and out they went.

On another night, she was awakened by a loud banging at the hotel door. It was young Mrs. Wilson from across the tracks, almost hysterical with fright. Her husband had come home, roaring drunk, threatening her, and she had run to the hotel for refuge. In a few minutes, the irate husband arrived, shotgun on shoulder, demanding his wife.

Ignored, he shouted louder and louder, and began walking around and around the hotel, shooting into the air at intervals. This was too much. Eyes flashing, mouth grim, Grandmother went to the door and called out, "Tom Wilson, put that gun down and go home to bed. Come back tomorrow sober and decent and you can have your wife back. Now get out!" The door slammed and Tom slunk off, presumably to do as he had been told.

Saturday nights were the "fun" nights. Nearly always, there was a dance in the hall over the general store, and what a commotion in the hotel when the sound of the piano and the tuning of the fiddle put everyone in a frenzy of preparation.

Before the girls could go to the dance, dishes had to be done, dining room swept, and milk put through the separator. These tasks were accomplished with incredible speed, and then came the wild scramble to get dressed: baths, curling iron, clothes borrowed from each other – all spurred on by the sounds of music and laughter across the way. Finally, late though they might be, they were ready.

Lucky in one way, at least. The orchestra could tune up, dancing could start in a desultory way, but the party couldn't get in full swing. There just weren't enough partners till the six Morgan girls got there!

Some people are old at 25, and others young at 80. Old age never quite caught up with Grandmother Morgan. She retained much of the vigor of youth and some of the vanities: cream massaged into her face at night, and 100 strokes of the brush on her black hair.

Many a time I heard her remark, "All the Morgans have nice legs," and then glance complacently at her own ankles, still slim and trim at 80. She must have been about 85 when she suggested to her daughters with whom she lived in Michigan that she had better buy a pair of galoshes before winter set in. They agreed, and offered to get them for her, or go with her, but she said she would go that morning by herself. That evening during dinner, one of the girls inquired, "Well, Mother, did you get your galoshes?"

"No," she replied disgustedly, "they made my

ankles look too thick."

Nor did her influence cease, even after her death (at age 92 in 1944). I know for a fact that many a decision is still made and a difficult course of action determined on the basis of, "Well, Mother Morgan would have done it this way."

As recalled by Ruth's son, David, here is a small boy's view of raising chickens on that Nebraska farm in the 1930's:

In the early 1920's, Mom and Dad were quite excited about the possibilities of what could be done with their 30 acre plot of rich bottom land there beside the Republican River. They had great plans; along with "truck gardening," as they called it, they would hatch high quality chicks from eggs, with the resulting hens producing premium eggs.

So they bought fancy white leghorns – Tancreds. They sold the chicks locally, for customers to raise to adult status, providing plentiful eggs and tender poultry. They called their business "The Bostwick Hatchery," and even had printed letterhead stationery.

The business seemed to get off to a good start. The chicks were hatched in early spring in the incubators in the storm cellar they had built, and then sold. They kept some chicks for raising for the next season's production, hoping to have a reasonable self sustaining condition, with only occasional new purchases from sources in Oregon.

What could be better? Well, for starts, Dad's customers could have paid for the chicks they bought in a reasonable time. There were great expectations; it was the '20's, and credit abounded. Buy some chicks on time, raise them to become layers, sell the eggs, pay off the bills. Then the depression loomed. Money got short, and the operation ground to a halt.

I was born in 1924, so wasn't in on the early heady days, but in the '30's, they were still growing chicks, though on a less grand scale than hoped. Dad tracked the individual hen's laying by leg-banding them for identity, then trapping them when they went into the nests to lay eggs. They tripped a little door shut with their tails. In this manner, he could identify the best layers and select them and their eggs for future production.

As a small boy, it was my job to water, feed, clean up after, and collect eggs. There was a side issue that got in my way, however: those select big white Oregon roosters that were a necessary part of the egg and chick production process.

These roosters had spurs, not just average, domesticated chicken spurs, but monster spurs, it seemed to me. Spurs three to four inches long, with a vicious curve to pierce and rip, and the roosters had the nerve to take on all perceived interlopers, large or small, who dared to invade their pen domain.

To a small boy, it seemed to me all they ever did was eat, make a lot of noise crowing and flapping wings, and try to spur me when I was least expecting it. If I spied an egg that a hen had laid under a secluded overhang, this meant I had to get down on my hands and knees to collect it. That was the time for the "white flash" to strike.

In an instant, he would catch me from behind, spurs foremost, while also slamming me with his wings and beak. Ouch, if he could get a spur into my posterior, all the better. This was his territory, and I had better learn it, and exit in a hurry.

Once in awhile, a shout would not be enough to stop him, so I would have to back out and chase him off. If he was feeling particularly mean, he might have one last go at me before running off to hide behind the hens for another day. After the chase, I would have to stop, assess the damage to my backside, decide whether I should complain to the Management – Mom – or just wait for an opportunity to get even. He was faster than me, so I would have to corner the beast to swat him, not an easy thing to do.

One time, the sovereign of all, Dad, was down on all fours, cleaning out under a roost, when up behind him strutted Mr. Rooster, head down, curved tail *feathers in full spread, wing at the droop, in full battle position. He was blind to Dad, of course, and the rooster had the added advantage of using the nearby cackling hens for cover.*

Dad was an ample target, not to be ignored. In a second, up in the air Mr. Rooster bounded, spurs to the fore, pressing the attack. The spurs easily penetrated the blue denim and struck red meat. Dad whirled around just as the bird was on his second slashing attack, and struck Dad square in the face. Into his cheek went the spear, and out went a tooth.

If Dad could have caught that bird just then, I think there would have been chicken in the pot for dinner that night.

Dad cooled off when he remembered that he would have to buy another expensive rooster as a replacement, and the new one would be just as mean. There are some things that just had to be endured. The rooster was king in his pen, and that was that.

DATES RELATING TO EVENTS IN RUTH'S STORY:

1854 – Kansas-Nebraska Act opens 50 million acres of grassland in Kansas alone, available for taking by "staking a claim."

1862 – Homestead Act specifies that 160 acres of federal land is deeded to any "head of household" who improves the land within 6 months, lives there 5 years to "prove up" his/her land.

1854 to 1890 – 3 waves of migration westward, motivated by slave vs. free state controversy, by the "rags to riches" American dream, and the desire for a fresh start.

1877 – the Morgans (from our story) arrive in Kansas with 4 children, in a covered wagon.

1894 – Ruth Morgan Smith born, following a move across the Nebraska border for "better education.

1913 – 1918 – Ruth graduates from Superior High School in Superior, Nebraska, teaches in a country school, goes to college one year at Northwestern University, spends a summer with Chautauqua, where she meets, and then marries Luther Edward Smith in 1918.

1929 – Stock market crash.

1932 – Bank closings mean there is not enough gold in the Federal Reserve to back the currency.

1935 - Republican River flood, following years of depression, dust storms, drought and grasshoppers, demolishes Smith farm and many others.

1933 through the 30's – President Franklin Roosevelt launches the New Deal, which helps the Smiths:
CCC – Civilian Conservation Corps
        rebuild their home.
FERA – Federal Emergency Relief Administration
        with funding after the flood.
PWA – Public Works Administration
WPA – Works Progress Administration
        rebuild their home.
AAA – Agricultural Adjustment Act
REA – Rural Electrification Administration
        get electricity in 1950.
        Social Security
        helped Ruth in her later years.

1941 – 1945 – U.S. in World War II.

May 5, 1945 – VE Day: Allied victory in Europe.

July 16, 1945 – another flood hits the Smiths

Aug. 6, 1945 – Atomic bomb dropped on Hiroshima.

Aug. 14, 1945 – Japan decides to surrender.

Aug. 15, 1945 –Emperor Hirohito's radio address makes it official.

Sept. 1, 1945 – Jane Smith marries Howard Yeremian in Boise, Idaho.

Sept. 2, 1945 – Japan signs treaty on U.S.S. Missouri.

A FEW "DATED" EXPRESSIONS IN RUTH'S STORY:

"I envy the woman with orderly bumps on her head."
A reference to the once popular "phrenology," a system thought to be able to identify character traits by studying the shape of bumps on the skull.

"We used feed sacks for sheets."
In the 1930's and 40's, feed companies began putting out sacks with pretty prints on them. Women used them to make aprons and tablecloths. (I know. I did it. V.S.)

"...kitcat to be varnished."
As Dave recalls, they referred to a tall storage cabinet in the kitchen as a "kitcat."

"War time"
Before daylight saving time, there was war time, the same idea – to lengthen the light time of the working day, in this case, for both war workers in defense plants

and farmers.

"Our Navy cadet sends his laundry home."
This was common in colleges, too, during this period, since there were no automatic laundry facilities until after the war. Laundry cases were heavy cardboard or stiff-sided cases, with straps to hold them shut, mailed at special low-postage rates. (If you were lucky, Mom put a bag of cookies in with the clean clothes – IF she had enough sugar-ration stamps to bake them).

"Oh, how I hate ironing white shirts!"
No wonder. Until they got electricity in 1950, Ruth had to not only starch and dampen the shirts, but had to iron them by heating the iron on their old wood-burning stove.

"black oilcloth mourning..."
You got us! We know she meant mourning would cease when Japan surrendered and the war was over, but "oilcloth?"

LOOK UP AT THE HAWKS

ACKNOWLEDGMENTS TO THOSE WHO HAVE HELPED IT ON ITS JOURNEY

Forty years have passed since Ruth Morgan Smith gave me her writings and asked me to "Do something with these, Vivian." What happened to those writings since then is something of a story in itself and one that neither she or I could have planned or imagined.

She had trusted me with her very personal responses to a troubled place and time in our country's history, and the challenge was a little frightening. She was writing, not through the haze of nostalgia, but in the midst of the events themselves. The very thing that gave her writings such freshness and immediacy was also what made them so difficult to arrange. She had written randomly, as the events were happening, on the backs of Department of Agriculture envelopes, torn scraps of paper, a spiral journal, whatever happened to be available at the moment. I noticed several pages were addressed as letters to her mother, who so obviously served as a role model for Ruth, and I decided this might be the thread to bind them together.

My supportive husband of sixty three years, Ruth's son, Dave, deserves a special thank you for his role in telling this story. Not only did he also live through those times, but without his encouragement as consultant, fact checker, errand runner, and patient computer coach, this story might never have been finished.

Ruth's other three children, Jane, Betty, and Luther, also helped me to fill in details where they were sparse. Jane and her "new hubby," Howard Yeremian, owned a music business in California, and since Howard's death, Jane has been living with one of her three children, Kathy and her husband, Duke Clarke. They are currently located in California. Betty and Jake Kindscher brought up their seven children on their farm in Nebraska not too far from Bostwick. Betty has remained on the farm since Jake's recent death. Luther retired from his career as an engineer designing industrial plants and lives with his wife, Paige, in the home they designed and built on the Chesapeake Bay in Virginia. Their four sons and their families are all located on the east coast. David retired from the Naval Air Systems Command in Washington, D.C. and we remain in our home in northern Virginia, with all three of our children in the immediate area.

We were delighted to have some of our dates verified by "Morgan," a family history published by a relative we have never met, Harvey James Morgan in Seattle, Washington.

Our initial intention was simply to have a story to pass along to the family, and I gave it to our daughter,

Debi, to read. Our children had known their grandmother through our visits to Nebraska, but primarily during her later years. Suddenly Debi had a different picture of her grandmother, as a young, vital woman stepped from the typewritten pages. As a singer/songwriter, Debi responded in the way that seemed natural to her, by writing songs based on her grandmother's words.

It was at this point that Ruth's story seemed to take on a life of its own, and I would like to acknowledge a number of the people who helped it on its way. One of my daily morning-walk companions, Pat Barron, said, "Vivian, you've got to do a program on this!" As an artist, Pat was a member of the Washington Women's Art Center in Washington, D.C. and they set a date for a performance there on November 4, 1979. I arranged cuttings from the story into readings interspersed with the songs Debi had written. We continued to do the program around the D.C. area after that first performance.

When Dave and I attended a series called "Portraits in Motion" at the Smithsonian's National Portrait Gallery, I wondered if it might be a setting appropriate for "Look Up at the Hawks," so I contacted Ken Yellis, the Gallery's Director of Education. He decided to take a chance on these unknowns, and booked us as part of the Gallery's "Look Back at the FDR Years" in February, 1982.

Fortune smiled on Ruth's story once again. Richard Harrington gave the program a nice mention in the "Washington Post," and the weather in February was good that winter. It seemed that every displaced Nebraskan in the D.C. area came out, and two extra performances were added, all with standing room only.

"Hawks" was given another boost when National Public Radio's "All Things Considered" gave it coverage, followed by an interview with Susan Stamberg. There was another on "Radio Smithsonian," and one with Ken Bader on "Voice of America." What joy to have friends in Africa and India say they had heard the program.

Senator Carl Curtis had been at the Smithsonian performance; he and several alumni of Nebraska colleges suggested we take the program on tour to the Midwest. We found that it might be eligible for grants to assist in financing such a tour. We will always be grateful to the state and national Arts and Humanities organizations that help make programs like this available.

Our daughter, Megan, had recently graduated from college, and accompanied us on our tour with her saxophone. She and Debi sometimes preceded "Hawks" with songs from the 1930's - songs like "Blue Moon" and "Happy Days are Here Again." We thank our son, Douglas, a computer programmer, for keeping up the home front while we toured.

One Midwestern performance had special meaning for us. The Nuckolls County Historical Society, with Chauncey Mickelson as our contact person, sponsored a performance at Superior High School, where Ruth had graduated in 1917. "The Superior Express," edited by Bill Blauvelt, gave us so much publicity we felt like visiting celebrities.

The Nebraska State Historical Society lent us much encouragement, and while in Lincoln, Nebraska Educational Television did a half hour special on our program, produced by Gary Hochman. Our thanks, too, to all those Midwesterners who attended our performances and shared with us their memories so similar to Ruth's.

Unfortunately, Ruth Morgan Smith died, a victim of Alzheimer's, in 1978. We like to think that she would have been as pleased and amazed as we were that all this had fallen into place, and that her words from those Nebraska prairies had been heard around the world.

As for what happened to "Hawks" since the 1980's, Debi's singing career involved more touring, currently with a women's group, "The Four Bitchin' Babes." We gradually cut back on performances. There were requests for a printed version, and we had some initial encouragement. A personal note from Charles Flowers, an editor at W.W. Norton's, agreed with our assessment that " the work of this particular 'closet writer' is more appealing and accomplished than most," but indicated the work was probably not long enough for book publication. I did not persist, and we moved on to other interests.

Why now? Why have we come back to this? Today's world in many ways faces challenges similar to those of Ruth's in the 1930's, making her story perhaps more relevant than ever. Computer technology and self-publishing have made strides since the early 80's, so Debi has taken to her keyboard and declared, "Mom! It's time! We've got to do this." Without Debi's urging and hard work, this book would not, even now, have happened.

Thank you to all, named and unnamed, who helped "Look Up at the Hawks" along the way. Here, forty years later, is Ruth Morgan Smith's story, finally, in print.

A few personal thoughts:

During these past forty years, I have often considered the effect Ruth and her writings have had on my own life and ideas. Ruth's words may have been relatively few, but they say so much.

Why did Ruth take the time from her busy life on the farm to write all these things down? My belief is that in her heart of hearts, Ruth was a writer who simply had to write; she had, indeed, submitted material to several magazines of the day. And she *knew, along with journal writers through the years, that putting things on paper is a way to deal with the challenges of the day.*

People have asked - and I have wondered myself - why Ruth gave the writings to me, a daughter-in-law, rather than to a member of the family. My guess is that her own family was emotionally involved and still recovering from those days of hardship. She knew I was overwhelmed and intrigued by the downright courage it took to face life on those Nebraska prairies, so very different from the lush green rolling farmland in Wayne County, Ohio, where I grew up. (Dave never lets me forget that I'm from what he calls "the land of milk and honey.") She also knew that I had taught English, speech and drama, and was doing freelance writing at the time.

Working on Ruth's story has lent new enthusiasm to my own love of story-telling. I am drawn particularly to so often untold stories of women. Stories of families, neighborhoods and communities await someone to tell them. For initiating and fostering my interest, I would like to add a note of appreciation to my own family:

To my grandmother, Effie Hauenstein Douglas, who died when I was only 10 years old, but left me with memories of being spellbound by tales of the pranks she and her siblings played when they were children on their Ohio farm. "Tell tricks, Grandma!" I begged, "Tell tricks." How I wish we'd had tape recorders then.

To my mother, Edna Moser Douglas, who read to me nightly when I was small. With great trepidation, she confessed to my dad during some very lean years in the 1920's, that she had ordered a set of books with classic stories for children. And thank you to my father, Lee Henry Douglas, who was a teacher and born story teller: he pronounced the purchase of the books a great idea. I still have those well-worn books, along with another childhood favorite, his 2-volume set of "Poems Teachers Ask For."

No time to read to children in this over scheduled high tech world today? There's no time not to. And the time spent writing or recording your family story, or even special parts of it (family recipes, perhaps), may be some of the most important time you will ever spend.

--Vivian Douglas Smith, 2012

Many thanks to my Grandmother Ruth for writing down her thoughts and observations and sharing them with us... I continually find inspiration in her appreciation for life's little blessings, even in the face of some of life's greatest challenges. Thanks to my mom for seeing the beauty in Ruth's words, and for taking the time to put her story together so coherently... collecting information, writing, and filling in missing pieces. Thanks to my Dad for being our ever generous,

support and presence, as well as to my siblings, Megan and Doug. Thanks to Kendra Chilson for technical assistance with the photographs and book cover, and to Diana Pinkham and Unity for providing the 'spark' that started me working on this beautiful project again. Finally, thanks to my own family, Michael and Lee, for lovingly allowing me the time and space to make this publication possible, and to the Smith family for their remarkable story and spirit.

--Debi Smith Jaworek, 2012
(http://www.DebiSmith.com)